P-51 MUSTANG
RESTORED

Paul Coggan

Motorbooks International
Publishers & Wholesalers ®

First published in 1995 by Motorbooks
International Publishers & Wholesalers, PO Box 2,
729 Prospect Avenue, Osceola, WI 54020 USA

Motorbooks International is a certified trademark,
registered with the United States Patent Office

The information in this book is true and complete
to the best of our knowledge. All recommendations
are made without any guarantee on the part of the
author or Publisher, who also disclaim any liability
incurred in connection with the use of this data or
specific details

We recognize that some words, model names and
designations, for example, mentioned herein are
the property of the trademark holder. We use them
for identification purposes only. This is not an
official publication

Motorbooks International books are also available
at discounts in bulk quantity for industrial or
sales-promotional use. For details write to Special
Sales Manager at the Publisher's address

Library of Congress Cataloging-in-Publication Data
    Coggan, Paul A.,
    P-51 Mustang restored/Paul A. Coggan.
        p. cm—(Enthusiast color series)
    Includes index.
    ISBN 0-87938-991-5 (pbk.)
    1. Mustang (Fighter planes)—Maintenance and
        repair. 2. Airplanes—Conservation and
        restoration. I. Title. II. Series.
    TL685.3.C564   1995
    623.7'464'0973—dc20   95-6119

On the front cover: The *Lil' Margaret* in her
element. The addition of wartime accessories like
guns, camera, and fuselage fuel tank set this
warbird restoration apart. Edward Toth, Jr.

On the frontispiece: A decade of hard work comes
to fruition as Butch Schroeder climbs aboard *Lil'
Margaret* for his first flight. Paul Coggan

On the title page: Lil' Margaret in all her glory,
complete with markings. Edward Toth, Jr.

On the back cover: Top: The replica Browning
.50cal guns are wired, although they cannot fire.
Mike VadeBonCoeur Bottom: [Back 1] Butch
checks out the fit of the cowling. Mike
VadeBonCoeur

Printed and bound in Hong Kong

Contents

Acknowledgments

Many people have helped in the preparation of this book. I would like to thank Henry "Butch" Schroeder most of all for the time he has taken to encourage me to write the book and to get the story straight. I have come to know him very well and he is the most mild mannered, and modest warbird owner I have ever met. I have been rewarded greatly by his friendship and fascinated by his determination. Butch has the ability to make a major problem seem like a minor irritation, when many of us would tear around in a mad panic. Thanks, Butch.

I also feel privileged to call Mike Vade-BonCoeur a friend. We have had many interesting trans-Atlantic telephone calls to sort the details in completing the story of this remarkable project. Also, during the rebuild Mike had the foresight to take the many photographs and note interesting details, without which this book would not have been possible. Also my thanks to John Dilley, President of Fort Wayne Air Service, for the time taken to write about the test flight flying. John has been involved with Mustangs for longer than anyone else I know and is the perfect gentleman—certainly a worthy ambassador for the warbird movement.

Special thanks to Philip Warner who has accompanied me on my globe trotting and Mustang viewing over the years. We have shared many a joke and many an arduous journey on our forays into Europe and the United States in search of stories (and Harvard parts!).

Last, but not least, to the three ladies this book is dedicated to: Butch's wife Debbie, Mike's wife Beth, and my own Amanda. They all have experienced the absentee husband syndrome—whether we were "down at the hangar" or in front of the word processor. And all because of the other lady in our lives—that pesky North American Mustang.

Introduction

Butch Schroeder, F-6D
1993 Grand Champion, World War II Category
Experimental Aircraft Association/Warbirds of America
Oshkosh, Wisconsin

So Butch realized his ambition to win first place at the Experimental Aircraft Association's (EAA's) 1993 convention in the World War II warbird stakes. Just a few weeks earlier at Danville, Illinois, on June 17th at 1701 John Dilley, the President of Fort Wayne Air Service took to the air for the first time in the newly rebuilt North American F-6D—the photo reconnaissance version of the Mustang; the aircraft's first flight since 1949. John made an hour-long test flight during a break of clear weather between fierce thunderstorms, landed with a big grin on his face, and pronounced *Lil Margaret* a beauty. This was the first post-restoration warbird flight I'd ever seen, and it was rather special. For the twelve years that Butch, Mike and Dave had toiled on the project I had kept in close contact.

Butch and I had talked at least twice a month and he had told me about the chase for the parts; some were easy to find because not all the Mustang operators were using them—armor plate for example—but others were more difficult. Cowling frames and cowlings were difficult to get. I'd also had first hand experience of the way Butch operated in his quest to complete the jigsaw. In 1989 I had been invited to fly to Oshkosh, Wisconsin, in Butch's other P-51D, a tall-tailed Cavalier Mustang. En route Butch told me we had to find Watertown—he owed someone a big favor for locating some of the F-6D camera gear for him. To cut a long story short we found Watertown and I climbed out of the back seat to make way for a special gentleman receiving his well-earned reward—a few circuits in the Mustang! I was also lucky enough to share some of Butch's contacts in the Mustang world. And over the months I shared some of his anxieties about the length of time the project was taking. Nevertheless, Butch and Mike had restored a beautiful T-6 in between commencing work on the F-6D and completing it. The Texan had won the reserve Grand Champion warbird award at Oshkosh. Without doubt the most sobering moment of all, and one of the most momentous days in my life in aviation, was that stormy June day when the Mustang took to the air for the first time. For the rest of the day Butch was reserved and a little withdrawn. The following day, amidst a small crowd of friends and well-wishers, he calmly strapped himself into the Mustang and taxied out to the threshold at Danville for his maiden flight.

So N51BS had flown. It had always been Butch's ambition to win the coveted Experimental Aircraft Association/Warbirds of America "Grand Champion" warbird award at Oshkosh and the following weeks were to see the final push after years of hard work, searching for parts, fitting the myriad of stock items you just don't see on Mustangs in the nineties (including some of the camera gear), polishing, detailing all the stencils, and painting the nose art. I well remember receiving Butch's first letter telling me how he would rebuild his second Mustang—and how it would emerge "just as it did from the North American factory." At the time, I didn't know him terribly well and recall thinking, "Who is this guy?" To those who do know him, it was no surprise that he won the award. Though three people and a small number of specially selected subcontractors had worked tirelessly toward this

goal, Butch would be the first to admit that without the enthusiasm and dedication shown by Mike VadeBonCoeur it would have taken much longer to rebuild the aircraft.

At the time of writing there are approximately 158 airworthy Mustangs flying around the world with another eight or so on rebuild. Out of all of these what makes N51BS so special?

When Butch Schroeder acquired the airframe from Bill Myers at Baldwin, Missouri, in 1981 it was unique in that it had never been rebuilt since the day it rolled out of the North American factory in Dallas, Texas. It even had the original makers plate in the cockpit, fastened in the very place a North American factory worker had riveted it.

That may not seem anything out of the ordinary until you consider that some of the flyable Mustangs have been rebuilt many times—twice, three, or even four times due to a number of factors. The majority of today's airworthy P-51s come from either ex-Royal Canadian Air Force stocks (the RCAF surplused their aircraft in the mid-fifties) or from third world air force stocks. The last air arm to surplus the Mustang was the Fuerza Aerea Dominicana which phased out nine airframes and many tons of spares in the mid-eighties. The Dominican Mustangs had been rebuilt many times in military service both shortly after they were acquired from Sweden and again much later under U.S. Government military aid programs. So these aircraft had undergone military upgrades and modifications that moved the aircraft away from their 1944 stock configuration.

The civilian Mustangs are modified and rebuilt because of personal preference, wear, and accidents. Warbird owners modify their planes with everything from more comfortable interiors to air racing bits. Accidents take a toll on the planes, as well. Some aircraft required little more than cosmetic repairs while others required major surgery; complete dismantling, fuselage inserting in a jig, and straightening out with new extrusions. Some also required new wings building (Cal Pacific Airmotive of Salinas, California have built more than forty sets of new P-51 wings since the company started up).

The F-6D *Lil' Margaret*, however, had not been modified since it was phased out of service in 1949. The Mustang could have been in a time capsule as it sat in a garage in Missouri. Though this aircraft would not have appealed to many potential owners (most prefer aircraft that fly) it was ideal for Butch. In 1981, rebuilding warbirds to original condition was not as fashionable as it is today. In lots of ways, Butch and his team were pioneers. They were not the first to restore a warbird to its original condition, but they were the first team to incorporate absolutely everything—armor plating, guns, the fuselage fuel tank, and so on—into the restoration.

The end result is a flying museum piece that evokes a lot of emotion in the people who flew Mustangs during World War II and Korea. Butch has heard, "This is just how I remember it..." many times. I suspect it gives Butch great pleasure.

So here starts the story of this remarkable airplane and Butch Schroeder's quest for the most complete and original flyable Mustang...

Chapter One

The Men and their Mustang

The story of *Lil' Margaret* began in 1981. Henry "Butch" Schroeder acquired the disassembled but eighty percent complete airframe from Bill Meyers of Baldwin, near St. Louis, Missouri. It had never been on a civil aircraft register before.

Butch explains how he tracked down the airframe. "There had been many rumors going around—even before I purchased the Cavalier—that a stock, almost complete Mustang had been put in storage in St. Louis, Missouri. I had talked on a number of occasions with Bill Simms who had told me about the airplane, but no matter how hard we tried we could not track the owner down. In the end Bill Simms introduced me to some friends of his who knew the owner and it was agreed I should be allowed to go and see it," Butch said.

The immaculate Lil' Margaret *is the result of a ten-year restoration project initiated by the determination of Henry "Butch" Schroeder and completed with countless hours of labor by Butch and his crew.* Edward J. Toth, Jr.

Butch subsequently purchased the airframe and, in five trailer loads, the Mustang was transported to Vermilion County Airport at Danville, Illinois, which would be its home for the next twelve years before it took to the air again.

With the aircraft back at Danville, Butch began to plan the rebuild. It was not a short-term project, for Butch had decided that this rare airplane (there were only two other F-6 Mustangs known to exist) would be completely restored, using as many original parts as possible. "As soon as I saw it I knew this was the project I needed to build what I felt would be the ultimate representation of a World War II fighter," Butch said. The intent was that the restored Mustang would be identical to the aircraft that came off the production line at North American Aviation's plant in Dallas, Texas. To undertake such a project requires hard work and dedication as well as a significant injection of cash and contacts.

At times, progress seemed remarkably slow to Butch, as it does to most hands-on rebuilders. For every hour spent actually

Back home with the trophy that represents the realization of an ambition Butch held for nearly twenty years. Behind him sits one of the world's *greatest warbird restorations, one which many knowledgeable people in this field have said sets the standard for the future.* Edward Toth, Jr.

working on the airplane probably at least another three are spent on the telephone chasing hard-to-find parts and elusive rare items, particularly when an aircraft is being rebuilt to factory condition.

Butch told me why he took the trouble to rebuild the aircraft to original condition. "I felt I owed it to the airplane. Its uniqueness, and the fact that no one had rebuilt it

before, the rarity of the type attracted me to the idea of rebuilding the aircraft back to stock condition."

Butch owns Schroeder's Drive In, formerly the Burger Chef in Danville, Illinois. It was owned by his father before him. Butch has always been interested in warbirds and specifically in the North American Mustang. He began building a scale replica of the P-51 some years ago but after tiring of that he became involved with real warbirds and acquired his first F-51D, a tall-tailed Cavalier aircraft, in 1982 from Ward Wilkins. Since the F-6D has flown the aircraft was put up for sale just as this book was being written. Butch had also been involved with Mike VadeBonCoeur in the rebuild of his T-6D which had won the Reserve Grand Champion award at Oshkosh first time out.

Mike VadeBonCoeur took interest in *Lil' Margaret* from the start. He'd stop by the airport now and then and help on a volunteer basis. To cut a long story short Mike went to college, got qualifications as an A&P and then joined the project full time. Mike's input was vital to the project as you will see as the story unfolds…

These are the men who put together the warbird that won the 1993 World War Two Grand Champion Award. From left to right, the men are assistant crew chief David Young, owner and pilot Butch Schroeder, and crew chief Mike VadeBonCoeur. After seeing years of hard work (an estimated 10,000 man hours) result in the award at the Oshkosh air show, these are three very happy men. Beth VadeBonCoeur

Part way through the project, Brigadier General Robin Olds, an 8th Air Force and Vietnam war ace visited the team at Danville, Illinois. Shown here with Mike VadeBonCoeur, it was a welcome morale booster when Olds declared the aircraft "just like the one I flew during World War II." Butch Schroeder

The gang gathers to celebrate a successful first test flight. From left to right are Mike VadeBonCoeur, John Dilley, Henry "Butch" Schroeder III, David Young, Henry Schroeder II, and Bob Young of Young's Airframe Repair. Paul Coggan

Left
The day after the first flight, Butch tries the Mustang on for size and heads out for his first flight. Poor old Mike looks on anxiously. Paul Coggan

The Man Who Flew the Original *Lil' Margaret*: Clyde B. East

When Butch Schroeder acquired the F-6D he immediately began to research the aircraft's history. The individual aircraft record card was pulled from Maxwell Air Force Base and Butch discovered that the most notable units the aircraft had served with was the 69th Tactical Recce. Group, 363rd Recce Sqn. at Brooks Field, Texas, and the 10th TRS at Pope Field. After some research, Butch found a photograph showing that the aircraft of this particular group were marked in quite an interesting paint scheme; blue and white checkered tail and nose trim, blue spinner, etc. During the stripping of the aircraft Butch and Mike had found some blue and white paint, which tied in with the aircraft's previous unit's markings. The 15th TRS were assigned to the 10th PRG on 31st April 1944, and to the 10th from the 69th TRG on 11th July 45 to 22nd November 1945.

A short time later Mike and his wife Beth were touring the flea market at Oshkosh when Beth saw a print of an F-6, with blue and white checks. After talking with artist Mike Machat it was determined

France, December 1944. The F-6C (a P-51C with camera equipment) was one of Clyde East's Mustangs.
Clyde B. East

Clyde B. East ready to launch in Lil' Margaret.

that the paint scheme would be ideal for application to '786—what is more, the pilot, Clyde East, was still alive. Without hesitation, Butch decided the aircraft should be painted in this way as a tribute to the 9th Air Force Ace.

Clyde B. East was born on July 19, 1921, in Pittsylvania County, Virginia and joined the Royal Canadian Air Force in June 1941. He graduated from flying school at Dunnville, Ontario in November 1942.

He was assigned to the 10th Tac Recon Group, and the 15th Tac Recon Squadron, in England in January 1944 and stayed with this unit until V.E. Day in Germany. During this time he flew over 200 combat missions destroying some 14.5 enemy aircraft, all in the air. When he returned to the United States in 1945 he remained in the USAAF. In June 1946 East was assigned to the 1st Recce squadron at 12th Tac Recon Squadron, flying RF-80s. He accumulated over a thousand hours jet time before being sent TDY to Korea in August 1950. Here he flew some 100 missions in RF-51s (redesignated F-6Ds and Ks) and RF-80s.

Before his retirement he had different command assignments in both RF-51 and RF-101 units. He was the commander of 20th Tac Recon Squadron at Shaw Air Force base when he retired from the United States Air Force in February 1965 with the rank of Lt. Col. and joined the Rand Corporation.

A historic day indeed. Clyde East prepares to take off to lead the final formation flight of the 15th TRS from Nuremberg in Germany, June 9th 1945. Clyde B. East

F-6D-10NA 44-14306 at Trier in March 1945.

Clyde's Kills

Ninth Air Force Ace Captain Clyde B. East, 10th PRG, 15th TRS 9th Air Force.

Victory List

1 Fw190	6 Jun 44
1 Me109	17 Dec 44
1 Me109	15 Mar 45
2 Me109	24 Mar 45
2 Ju 87	27 Mar 45
1 Fw190	4 Apr 45
1/2 Ju88	4 Apr 45
2 Ju87	8 Apr 45
1 Si204	8 Apr 45
1/2 He111	8 Apr 45

Chapter Two

Rebuilding the Wings and Fuselage

The North American Mustang was originally manufactured in five completely separate parts in the wartime factory, all to be assembled when each component part was totally finished. The five major sections were: the central fuselage section (including

The process began when Butch purchased this Mustang back in 1981. The plane had sat for many years in St. Louis, Missouri. The complete mainplane weighs in at around 1,800lbs. Butch Schroeder

cockpit); the rear fuselage (with empennage and tail feathers), two complete wing sections, and the forward fuselage section complete with engine. This approach to fighter construction not only resulted in lower overall production costs but meant that at Inglewood, California, at the height of Mustang production—the fighters were being put together at the rate of almost one per hour: an impressive achievement.

Mike and Butch approached the F-6D project in a similar fashion; they assembled pieces of the plane separately. They felt this would be the most efficient and trouble-free way to put the plane together. Butch decided to begin construction of the wings rather than the fuselage.

Wings

Mike VadeBonCoeur became involved with the project straight out of his A & P course. He had been interested in warbirds from an early age, particularly the Mustang, and living in Danville he had seen Butch's Cavalier flying around the local area. His association with Butch began when he volunteered to help clean the Cavalier, and as things progressed he helped Butch with routine maintenance and eventually with transporting the F-6D to Danville just before the project started. After getting his qualifications at college, Butch asked him to work on the project on a trial basis. The trial went well and Mike continued working on the aircraft, as well as the T-6D project that was completed in between the start and finish of *Lil' Margaret*.

He told me, "When I became involved Butch had already started on the project. The wings had been completely stripped out and there was a huge pile of parts on the shelves from them. The wings had all been painted internally—a lot of panels had been removed, gear castings were out and Bob Young had done some of the skin work already. So essentially the wings were just a shell waiting to go back together (rebuilders—amateur and professional—agree that progress on a fuselage is a greater morale booster than progress on wings!). When the weather turned we moved our attention to the wings, trying to get those fitted out and mated together the best we could. That was fairly easy. One of the more difficult things on the wing was installing the fuel tanks, although installation with the wings in a vertical position would have been ten times easier than with the aircraft sitting on its gear. We utilized unused but stock fuel tanks. Though they were not cracked they'd taken a bit of a set and so we had to introduce air to inflate them so the studs would line up and we could fit them properly. There are three or four studs on the top and the bottom of

Here it is! How many times have you heard about the Mustang in the garage? In the U.K. it's the Spitfire or Hurricane in the barn. It just goes to prove that the rumor you ignore turns out to be the one that is true. Butch Schroeder

A myriad of spare parts were stored in the basement of the house including a spare canopy and several other major parts, all of which had rested in St. Louis since 1949. Butch Schroeder

The engine section of the Mustang weighs in at 2,200lbs less spinner and propeller. Here the bare Merlin is loaded onto the trailer with much huffing and puffing. Butch Schroeder

One of the five truck loads of Mustang to be transported to Danville, Illinois, and Vermilion County airport where the plane would spend the next twelve years before taking to the air. Butch Schroeder

each wing and all these have to line up at the same time, not to mention the filler caps and the fuel gauge—that was quite a trick! We kept our fingers crossed until the day we put fuel in it because I didn't want to have to pull those things back out!

"We continued with the wings to try and get them as far along as we could. I knew I didn't want to put any hydraulics in at that time—I felt it would be better as far as getting the right look was concerned for our custom-made lines and the wiring—to do this with the wings in the horizontal, working over my head. Although I ended up doing the wiring with the wing on the stand, the hydraulics were done working over my head, on a roll-around chair under the wings, after we'd mated the fuselage. We knew we had all the pieces and fittings to go back in the wings and that would keep us occupied until the following summer."

What else did they do before the fuselage and wings were mated together? Mike explained, "As much of the fitting of the gun bay doors, a lot of the internal brackets for the ammunition feed chutes and all the riveting was done with the wings on the stands. We even painted the wings in this position. This is often a point of fierce debate—many rebuilders wait until the aircraft is all together and then paint it. I'm not sure what we'd do if we did this again though. Of course you always run the risk of nicking or dinging the airplane during assembly after painting but we used protective tape to cover the wings, at least the leading third. I'd cover it all if I went through the process again."

The whole idea on this airplane was to make it as original as possible. Mike pointed out that the only deviation was in the use of some of the higher quality paints.

Although some people do not consider IMRON a true representation of zinc chromate, it is a lot easier to clean and maintain and Mike and Butch wanted to protect their investment.

Assembling the Fuselage

The F-6D Mustang fuselage is, apart from the camera ports, identical to a standard P-51D. The fuselage is built around four main extrusions which bolt to the firewall at the front and go in a tapering shape to the transport joint to the rear of the cockpit, attached to a shelf in the rear fuselage and all joined together in a two-piece fuselage rim at the transport joint. Over the years the four main extrusions take the strain and stress put upon the aircraft and are often subject to internal intergranular corrosion. At first glance, the extrusions can look perfect, yet a detailed examination will reveal the corrosion, which resembles gray metallic powder. The majority of rebuilt Mustangs have seen these four integral units replaced, and California-based metallurgist John Seevers had a batch made to original specifications. The extrusions in N51BS were replaced (for safety reasons) with new extrusions from John Seevers.

Butch Schroeder tries the Mustang out for size. It was always his aim that the aircraft would be rebuilt to stock condition, and that he would fly it. Butch already owned a Cavalier Mustang "North American Maid."

The completed wing section, minus wing tip sections, up on trestles for inspection. The mainplane still had the original U.S. markings; the *black marks are where the unit has been moved around on tires since put into storage in 1949.* Butch Schroeder

Attached to these extrusions are various frames throughout the length of the center section and the whole assembly is then metal skinned with sheet metal of varying thickness. The actual fuselage center section is 173in long and weighs in at 1,650lbs, dry (including canopy, oil tank, fuel cell, radio equipment, coolant radiator, air scoop, but less the rear tail cone.) To this main assembly are attached the three sections of air scoop (the center unit of which is known as a doghouse) which contain the coolant radiator and a lot of complex duct-

Left
An interesting shot showing the unrestored wheel well bays with the "plumbing" still in place. Note the surface corrosion and rusted ancillaries. Butch Schroeder

ing and internal metal shapes which are very difficult to reproduce.

Mike VadeBonCoeur describes how the project was tackled. "With the hangars at Danville having less than ideal space it was decided to strip the fuselage before the winter set in. Essentially this was to ensure we had enough work to keep us going through the winter months. Some of the fuselage parts were painted after cleaning and stripping out. But we were anxious to start on the rebuild of the fuselage! It was totally reskinned by Bob Young of Young's Airframe Repair before we stripped the remaining paint out of it, primed it and painted the insides. While the fuselage was being reskinned the extrusions were replaced. Also at this time the tail cone was painted internally—as much as possible. As Bob made the new skins I primed and

The same section shortly after paint stripping. Basically the wing skins were in excellent shape, though much of it was replaced with new metal at Young's Airframe repair.

24

Once inspected, the wings were split and some of the metal skins removed to reveal the inside. Note that enough skin remained on the wings to preserve the structural integrity of the unit. Butch found some very old candy wrappers in the wings as well as several autographs of the workers. Sadly, these could not be preserved.
Butch Schroeder

painted the insides of each one so over the winter he could put the new skins in place."

What about the items that separated the F-6D from a P-51D—the camera ports? Mike pondered, grinned and went on to explain, "Butch spent several years looking for them. Dennis Schoenfelder sent some of the ports from an ex-Israeli AF airplane in the early years of the project. When we received the Mustang the ports were just flush patched—covered up, though you could see where the patches were. We didn't

The wings were repaired where necessary, fitted with new skins, and painted. The original yellow zinc chromate paint was replaced with cockpit green; both were used by the factory.

Note the areas to be painted silver are masked off with newspaper and masking tape. Taping and masking is a laborious but vital task.

The port wing begins to come together as detailed parts are refitted. All new nuts and bolts to original military specification were used throughout the airframe.

Left
A smiling Mike VadeBonCoeur and David Young after the mainplane went back together without a hitch. The Mustang mainplane is joined in the middle by flanges on the wings which are bolted together.

have any mounts, nothing. The cable routing was modified inside the tail cone as well as the oxygen bottles and some of the hydraulic lines were re-routed from the standard pattern as well. Fortunately, all the internal fittings were still in place—in fact as related earlier the airframe was almost complete. Butch had the upper camera ports from Dennis but these were crunched. This was sent to John Neel at Georgia Metal Shaping. We were just tickled to death when we received the new

ones—and John had even straightened out the old one, which is usable again. We had to cut new glass and fit it to the ports as well."

By this time it was summer again. Mike continues, "We had practically a summer of stripping, cleaning, and repainting all of the fuselage parts we had removed from the Mustang. Again the cycle just continued where we inspect, clean, and paint so by the time fall rolls around we can put stuff back in the airplane. Fitting the fuselage went

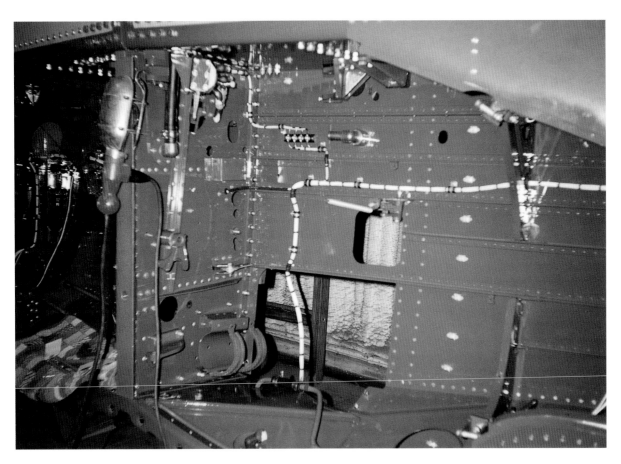

The wheel wells begin to come together. Following final painting, the electrics and new hardware are installed. Long hours spent checking *that every detail was correct and functional are a crucial part in preparing any warbird to fly.* Mike VadeBonCoeur

Left and Above
The doghouse section fits in between the forward shaped air scoop and the coolant radiator. The doghouse section is full of complex, curved metalwork, and is an absolute nightmare to recreate. The unit is shown prior to a complete tear down and rebuild. Mike VadeBonCoeur.

The doghouse section unit after being deskinned and disassembled. Each individual part was cleaned, repaired as required, alodined, etch primed, and reassembled before final painting. Mike VadeBonCoeur.

really well so the following summer we were able to start fitting final things like the rudder pedals.

"Butch spent a long time trying to get as many of the original parts for the airplane as possible. He was able to obtain the fuselage gas tank, the armor plate, and original radios. Fortunately, the radio/battery rack was still with the aircraft. Additionally we obtained the APS-13 tail warning radars which was a real coup, and the light assembly that goes on the upper left-hand windscreen—that's a pretty rare item. A friend of Butch's from the Air Force Museum said they do not even have one on their Mustang. The armor plate was also installed."

Butch and Mike discussed the idea of using aluminum to mock up the armor plate behind the pilot's seat and headrest, but in the end they decided to bear the

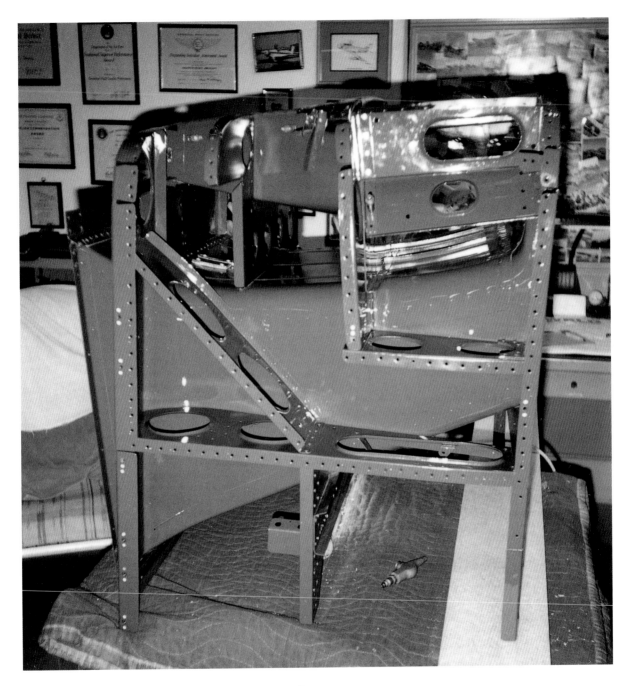

The doghouse gets the final coat of internal paint. Each subassembly was finished inside and out not just for cosmetics but for corrosion prevention as well.

The completed doghouse section is a work of art.
Mike VadeBonCoeur

weight penalty and use the original parts. Did they run into any real difficulties during fuselage assembly? "The installation of the armor plate and the fuselage fuel tank was interesting. The bolts for the plate lined up perfectly, and we collapsed the fuselage tank as per the manual for installation and it worked like a dream! It isn't airworthy and we have a plate behind the filler cap so no one can stick a fuel nozzle in

Right
Vertical fin complete, the area which is covered by the dorsal fairing is painted green. Georgia Metal Shaping did work on this unit. Mike VadeBonCoeur.

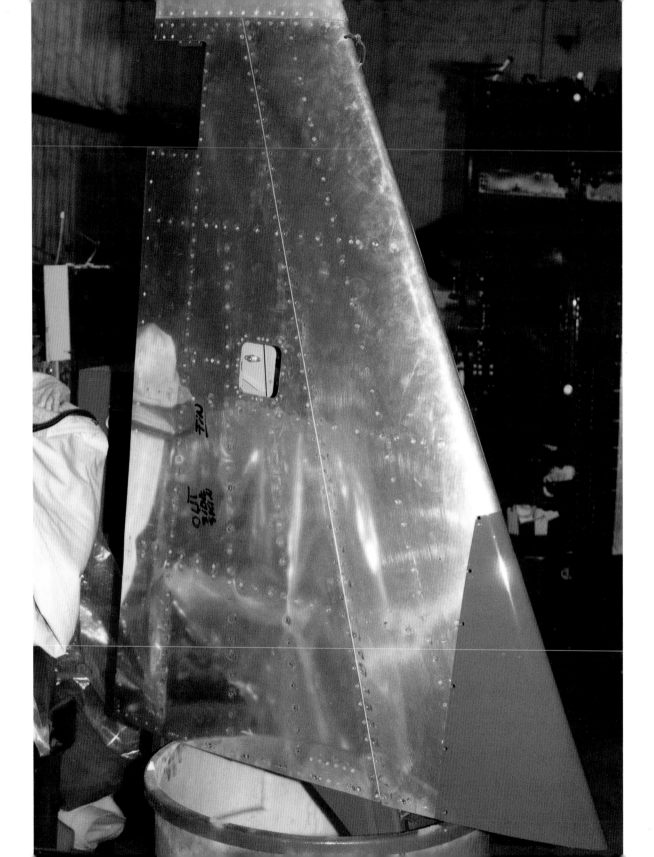

The cockpit before restoration commenced. The instrument panel has been stripped out for inspection and the whole area has extensive surface corrosion.

and try and fill it. The original seat also fit very well. All in all we were so fortunate that the aircraft was so stock to begin with and had never been civilianized." Mike goes to great pains to say, "I've got to hand it to the guys that put Mustangs together from parts—it's difficult enough fitting things that came out of the original airplane in the first place so heavens knows what it must be like fitting parts from other airplanes!"

Hydraulics

How did Mike feel as the first flight came ever nearer? "The hydraulic system was always the greatest personal concern to me. I'd never rebuilt hydraulic lines before and every hydraulic component in the aircraft was rebuilt. In the end it worked fine—we had a few leaks when we first put fluid in the system but that was to be expected. Fortunately, we have a hydraulic mule which we hooked up to the

Left
Patience is key to any restoration project. At times work seemed painfully slow to those involved. Here is the Mustang fuselage awaiting its turn in the rebuild process. Note the access hatch just to the rear of the cockpit canopy, also found on some ex-RCAF Mustangs. Butch Schroeder

The jigged Mustang fuselage. Note the four main extrusions were linked together by the fuselage ribs and then covered in a stressed fuselage skin. The extrusions were replaced by new units purchased from California metallurgist John Seevers. The work was undertaken by Young's Airframe Repair. Butch Schroeder

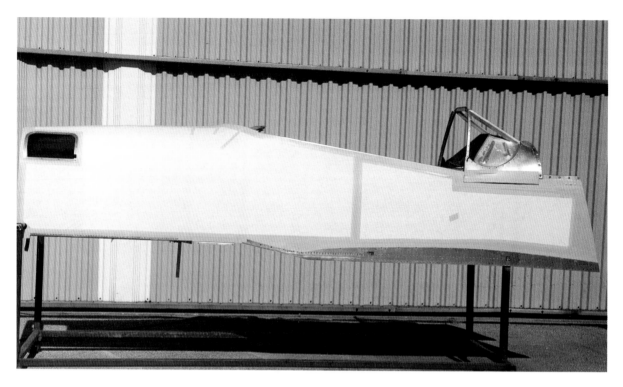

New extrusions in place, the fuselage had by this time been reskinned. It is shown here with the windscreen in place but not riveted in position.

Star Trek? No, Mike VadeBonCoeur dressed for action in the spray shop.

aircraft and ran for several hours before it flew. Again we did everything by the book and I had lots of advice from Gary Koepke and John Dilley at FWAS. Retraction tests were exhaustive, going through all of the scenarios in the manuals."

Radiator

What about the final testing prior to test flying? "We had purchased a radiator which had an old Pioneer Aircraft yellow tag with a 45psi pressure tag on it. Externally it looked good. We pulled the caps off and looked inside and it looked fine. Anyway, we decided to take it apart and detail

Though the factory finished the inside of the Mustang's fuselage in a semi-matte cockpit green, it is difficult to maintain. Butch elected to go for a gloss finish which is more easily cleaned and looks sharper. Mike VadeBon-Coeur

Right
The Mustang's windshield minus glass. Note the ribs on the actual instrument panel shroud. These are a good identity pointer for the later 25NA and 25NT Mustangs. Mike VadeBon-Coeur

The fuselage minus firewall after a first effort at polishing the skin. Most warbird rebuilders will tell you that rebuilding the fuselage is more satisfying than restoring the wings. Note the camera port on the side of the fuselage, near the tail.

John Neal at Georgia Metal shaping made a new one for N51BS from an original ex-Israeli Defence Force Mustang port supplied by Dennis Schoenfelder.

it ourselves with new gaskets etc. But when we had completed the unit and put it back together it just would not hold pressure. We asked Mike Nixon at Vintage V-12s for advice and he referred us to Dave's Radiator out in California. I had already overhauled the unit and had reached a dead end with the problem. After consultation with Butch I talked to Dave and he agreed to take a look at it and refurbish the unit. Some weeks later he mentioned it was the best Harrison radiator he had ever seen and probably it had never been on an aircraft! Dave knew it was the gaskets. On reflection we realized they had been hung on the wall here in the hangar for almost ten years! So Dave put new gaskets in, some new sealant, and did some approved modifications to the unit which included closing up some of the tubes, and building it up in various areas to beef it up. The radiator duly arrived, was plumbed in and

The frame for the engine cowling during construction. It is important for the cowling frames and cowlings to fit perfectly for a good-looking airframe. During World War II cowlings were individually fitted to each Mustang - and if cowlings were taken off and mixed up with other aircraft it resulted in ill-fitting units. Hence the practice of stenciling the last four digits of the aircraft's individual serial number on the outer skin of each cowling.

checked out and has worked very well ever since. We were very pleased with the work."

Engine

"For the engine runs again we had help from Fort Wayne Air Service (FWAS). As Mike Zolman at FWAS had rebuilt the engine he and John came over to Danville for the engine runs. They hooked up three oil pressure monitors. The engine started first time and was run for four and a half hours the first day and just over an hour the second day. Originally, this engine had never been in an airplane before. The engine was built by Packard, run on a test stand and then put straight into storage as a spare.

We asked Mike Zolman at FWAS what was entailed in rebuilding the engine. He told me, "Everything was in excellent shape. Basically it was simply a dismantling, inspection/testing, clean up, and

The engine cowlings were fitted after being cut, trimmed, and filed. Mike VadeBonCoeur

reassembly job...we had to inspect for corrosion, remove preservatives and generally prepare the engine for life in the Mustang again."

So how did this compare to an engine that had been run and was ready for overhaul? Mike told me, "Well, there were considerably less parts to replace. We followed the inspection procedures from the maintenance manual as we always do, though there was no corrosion and the engine was beautifully preserved, ripe for running. We also checked measurements of components

Right
Fitting the tail feathers. The vertical was rebuilt by Georgia Metal Shaping while the horizontal stabilizer is an original unit reskinned by Young's Airframe Repair. Note the wires from the Tail Warning Radar—a rare item indeed. Mike VadeBonCoeur

The radiator gave some cause for concern on its first pressure testing until it was realized that the gaskets, which had been hanging on the hangar wall for some time were probably no good because they were too old. Mike VadeBon-Coeur

to see if they were worn out, which in this case, due to the low running times they were not."

After each engine is rebuilt at FWAS it is standard procedure to install the engine in the aircraft in which they will fly and go through a standard ten-hour ground running program to break them in. After an hour or so the engine is stopped and checks are made. As the running time is increased, so are the power levels. If problems occur they are rectified and at this stage it is determined whether the engine needs more test time or not. The F-6D took to the air for the first time with just 6.7hrs on the engine.

So, with the fuselage approaching completion, plans were drawn up to join the fuselage and mainplane together and install the Merlin engine. It was to be a real morale booster.

The partly painted wings inside the hangar at Danville. The gun bays are masked off prior to painting. Mike VadeBonCoeur

Look at that shine! Polishing trials were undertaken very early on just in case things did not turn out and the aircraft fuselage needed to be painted. The NAA factory originally painted the fuselage rather than polished it and some disagreed with Butch and Mike's decision to polish Lil' Margaret. However you feel about the practice, there's no denying the polishing looks great. Note the aft house and very complex doghouse which were fitted prior to fitting the wings to ensure a perfect fit. Mike VadeBonCoeur

Chapter Three

Final Assembly and First Flight

At this stage the fuselage and mainplane were ready to be mated and the engine was ready for installation. But let's go back a few steps. I asked Mike VadeBon-Coeur about the way in which the F-6D was built up. Mike explained how they decided where to begin. "To be honest, when we were ready to start work I just didn't know where to begin, but we just thought about it logically, based on experience with other types—aiming to the point where when you install something you really do not want to take it out again. I also didn't want to close something up and not be able to get to it later. So, as an example, with the fuselage we put the hydraulic tank in first and start-ed building hydraulic lines and other things I knew I needed to go behind the instru-ment panel. I did the hydraulic plumbing first. I knew where the lines had to go, where the cables had to go, and the wiring

Another gorgeous air-to-air shot of Lil' Margaret. *Edward Toth, Jr.*

was really straightforward enough to route around that. We then bolted the tail cone in place. Then came the tail feathers and our dorsal fin. John Neal had made this—the one we had was in pretty poor shape and John took good care of it for us. All the fair-ings were unused stock parts, manufac-tured by North American Aviation—many of them still in their original wrappings. The majority of the fairings between the wings and the fuselage are also original NAA parts except what I call the elephant ear fairings and the front leading edge fair-ings—these were made by Dennis Schoen-felder out in California."

After some deliberation he went on to explain, "The separate fuselage was already painted on the inside so I wanted to get the rigging underway, or at least as much as possible before the mating of the two sub-assemblies was carried out. We heard this a lot from people like John Dilley—do as much as you possibly can before you put the two together, constantly. Of course, (as related earlier) this was the way North American did it in the factory. It was a

The mainplane is dragged out of the hangar on its custom-made stand ready for mating to the fuselage. Note the special markings on the upper wing surface which helped the pilot line up the aircraft for a particular photograph.
Mike VadeBonCoeur

temptation to put the two together as soon as possible because they look so good! However, I'm glad we resisted the temptation, for it became evident when they were mated how little room there was in the cockpit and the floor is angled so you have to constantly work against that, almost uphill, as well! By the time the two came together the engine mount was in place, and we had the oil tank installed. The firewall had everything in place. With the tail cone installed and all the cabling run—we couldn't complete the rigging until mating because the stick is attached to the mainplane..."

They were able to rig the rudder but didn't have the scoop, doghouse, or radiator installed. That was something everyone recommended they should do later even though North American assembled the fuselage and mainplane with them installed. The tail wheel gear was fitted and all the instruments installed in the panel. Mike knew where the radios were going. Basically then, the cockpit was finished.

With the aircraft almost complete what

The mainplane is lifted right side up and rested on a support.

The fuselage is then lifted onto the mainplane with the crane in the midst of a deluge.

Four bolts are inserted through castings in the fuselage lower longerons into castings in the wings.

Finally, bolts installed, the fuselage is lowered to the ground.

The Merlin engine, which had been rebuilt by Mike Zolman at Fort Wayne Air Service, was installed the same day as the wings and fuse- *lage were mated to make maximum use of the crane.* Mike VadeBonCoeur

were the final stages of preparation before it took to the air again? "Rigging the aircraft went quite smoothly and a lot of the credit again must go to John Dilley and Gary Koepke at Fort Wayne Air Service (FWAS). I had a hot line to them—they'd already done a lot of this type of work, and as I had lots of questions and needed advice I turned to them rather than muddle through or try and reinvent the wheel. Basically we did everything by the book, the best we could. We did change the flap travel by raising the flaps a little. We weren't getting the right fit between the trailing edge of the wing and the front of the flaps and we wanted to make sure that they looked right when they were up tight.

As we were making new fairings anyway we decided to adjust them to fit. Usually there's a few degrees drop on the flaps— some of the racers raise them up as well but we raised them even further and it looks good.

"Elevator and rudder were all straight-forward as was all of the trim rigging. I did have some problems trying to rig the rudder trim and the elevator trim because they changed the cable routing due to the camera position. We didn't have the original cables and there was no documentation anywhere that detscribes cable lengths, end types, etc. for the F-6D. Data was available for the P-51D but it was useless because of the cable re-route in the F-6."

For the major assembly a crane was hired (North American Aviation performed the work with the factory's huge load bearing gantry cranes). First of all the wings were pushed outside the hangar on their framework. The crane was maneuvered into position and then the complete mainplane, with the undercarriage extended and locked, was lifted out and supported underneath in the center. The fuselage was then lowered on to the mainplane, where it was attached with four large fuselage attach bolts which fit through the lower fuselage extrusions into the wing section. Mike described that glorious day when the wings and the fuselage were mated together. "At last we were ready to mate the two together. About a month after we painted the wings we were ready to go. We look back on that particular day and laugh. The crane was booked. We checked the weather—the trusty old Flight Service said the weather was forecast to get bad at about 1300—the time the crane was due to arrive, so we brought it forward. So we got everything outside in the morning, got the fuselage hooked up to the crane and guess what? The weather broke. We were drenched. By 1300 the weather had cleared and it was beautiful!"

One thing I had always wondered about was what happens if those four wing bolts didn't line up? After all the aircraft hadn't been together since the late forties! Did

The aircraft outside the hangar at Danville. Mating the wings and fuselage makes the plane look deceptively close to completion. A signifi- *cant amount of work remains to complete the project.* Mike VadeBonCoeur

they line up? Mike says, "Beautifully—we only had to do a little prying on the right rear, which is to be expected. From what we understand on some airplanes they have to get jacks between the two spars to spread them to make them fit!"

After the bolts had fit and were tightened up, the team took advantage of having a crane on site and fitted the Merlin engine. Remarkably, probably due to the intense and thorough preparation, it took just three hours to mate the wings and fuselage and install the engine. One thing that did require some thought was the lifting process. Almost always as a matter of course an aircraft suffers damage when it is being lifted by an inexperienced team as a result of chains not being padded, or correct lifting gear not being used. I once saw some aircraft transported out of a foreign country on the cheap. There would have been nowhere near as much costly damage done to the airframes if the owner had hired an experienced team. Short-term cash savings

Plumbing the engine is one of the many tasks necessary before Lil' Margaret *will fly. The cowling pieces were fitted before the engine was installed, and can be simply bolted up when the engine is hooked up.*

Some of the markings had already been applied when the aircraft was wheeled out into the sunshine for a photograph. The wing tip sections were still not fitted to the airplane at this stage. Items like bomb racks were installed at this stage. Mike VadeBonCoeur

can be much more expensive and time consuming in the long term!

Also of interest is the weight of the components. As an example, each wing panel (including landing gear, fuel tanks and wing tip section) weighs in at 900lbs. Each landing gear strut accounts for 200lbs of this weight. The center fuselage section (including fuel tank, oil tank, canopy, coolant radiator, and air scoop) weighs in at 1,650lbs. Plenty of experienced manpower, a good crane, and a knowledgeable operator are vital to the success of such an operation.

With the two main components and the engine assembled, the final rigging, wiring, and plumbing could be completed as well as the paint work finished, except for the nose art and stencils, before the aircraft flew for the first time. As related earlier, prior to the first flight everything was checked and double-checked. John Dilley had done extensive engine running to his satisfaction, and retraction tests had been carried

Plumbing and exhaust stubs installed, this shot shows the cowling support framework to advantage. Note the polished exhaust shrouds have also been fitted.

Wing tips installed, flaps down, and some paint work being completed. The aircraft is now looking more like a flyer every day! Mike VadeBon-Coeur

Cleaning and final painting begins. Note the new diamond tread tires and the silver/polished metal clam shell undercart doors as well as the new landing light. Mike VadeBonCoeur

out successfully. It was at this stage that I was planning a trip to the United States. Little did I know that both Butch and Mike had accelerated the program to the stage where the first flight was to take place during my visit...

First Flight

Come the day of the first flight Mike looked decidedly pale. I noticed someone shook his hand as soon as the aircraft got into the air but I could see that though he was confident of his ability he had a pained expression on his face—similar to the one expectant fathers have in the delivery room. Who could blame him? Afterwards Mike commented, "I was really nervous for the first flight. Despite the fact we had done all the requisite checks and functional checks I was still worried in case the hydraulics leaked or the wheels wouldn't come down". He need not have worried— and I was honored to shake his hand when John landed safely after the first flight. When the canopy rolled back John announced the baby was fit—and that Mike could have a job with him any time he liked.

We left Mike and Dave and Butch of course—for the owner put a lot of time and effort into the aircraft as well as that vital ingredient called cash—with just under a month to go before Oshkosh. A month in which all the final detailing and stenciling—had to be undertaken. In the end it was worth the effort—Butch had achieved his ambition.

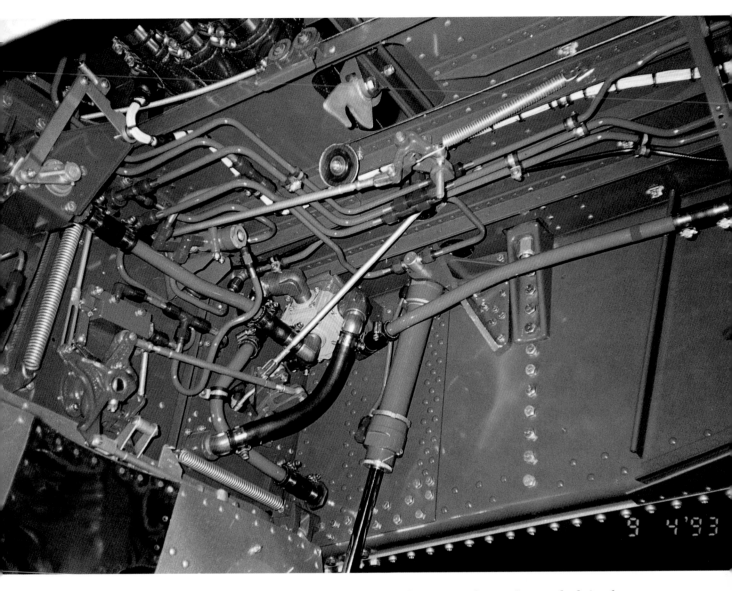

Wheel wells showing plumbing and wiring as well as the door rams. All new pipe work, hardware, and wiring looks exceptionally neat as does the new undercarriage uplock in the top center of the picture. Mike VadeBonCoeur

Another shot of the wheel well shows detail to advantage. Mike VadeBonCoeur

This photograph of the doghouse section shows why it is important to get this exact as it fits tightly up against the radiator with a complex ducting and pipe system. Note metal straps and castings hold the radiator unit in place. Again the advantages of using new hardware are evident in this photograph. Mike VadeBonCoeur

Mike Zolman (foreground) and Dave Young keep a watchful eye on the plane as John E. Dilley runs up the engine on May 25, 1993. Mike VadeBonCoeur

The plane was propped up on jack stands for retraction tests performed June 15, 1993. Mike VadeBonCoeur

The Test Flight
by John Dilley

Back in 1968 I stood in a garage in Baldwin, Missouri looking at a P-51 project. The owner wanted $12,000. I was willing to pay $8,000. Obviously, we couldn't come to an agreement.

About ten years ago I received a call from Butch Schroeder. He told me that he had found an airplane in a garage in the Midwest and that he had made a deal on the airplane and was going down the following week to bring it home. I said "Butch, I bet I can tell you where that airplane is located. It's in Baldwin, Missouri, in a garage; part of it is in the basement and part of it is in the back yard." He answered "How did you know that?" I then told him that, I tried to buy that aircraft in 1968 but was never able to complete the purchase.

As years went by, Butch started the restoration on it. I'd stop by from time to time to check on the progress. One day Butch asked me, "John, since we are going to have a new engine in this airplane and a totally rebuilt airframe, would you consider doing the test flying for me?" I told Butch I would have to think about it. Ten seconds later I told him, "Butch, I believe I could do that for you."

I grew more and more excited about test flying

After a final word with test pilot John Dilley, Butch forces as smile as he leaves John and the N51BS just prior to the airplane's first test flight. Paul Coggan

Bone dome on and oxygen mask in place, John taxis N51BS out to the end of the Danville runway for final checks, run ups, and eventual first flight. Paul Coggan

the Mustang, as I observed the quality of workmanship and that the aircraft was being put back to a 100 percent original condition. I thought that it would be quite an honor to test fly this magnificent Mustang for the very first time.

Then the time came to install the engine, previously overhauled in our shop at Fort Wayne Air Service. I went over on the day that they were ready to start the engine for the very first time and did the initial running. Everything checked out quite well.

About two months later I received a call from Butch stating that they had all the run in time on the engine and they were ready for the first test flight. He had also mentioned that Paul Coggan was coming from England to observe the test flight and take some photographs of the aircraft.

On the morning of the agreed date, I hopped into our Cessna 210 and headed for Danville. The weather was gorgeous in Fort Wayne, Indiana, but as I got closer to Danville it became darker and darker. There was a line of thunderstorms right across Danville so I had to make a decision whether to disappoint them and return to Fort Wayne, or try to find a way around the nasty weather. I chose the latter and flew about forty miles on to the north and then west to enable an approach to Danville airport from the west. It was still raining lightly at the airport when I landed.

I could see the smiles on the faces of Butch, Paul, and Mike as I walked up to the hangar in anticipation of the very first flight. We kidded a little to calm our nerves while we looked the airplane over from top to bottom looking at all the trim tabs because on the Mustang it's so easy to get them

The tail comes up as N51BS stabilizes before getting airborne. As if by magic, the sun shone for the only time that afternoon as John lifted off the Danville runway. Paul Coggan

After a squawk-free test flight John Dilley puts N51BS back on the ground. Paul Coggan

reversed. We then checked the movement of all the controls and systems to insure they were properly serviced.

The weather finally broke and the time for the first flight was at hand. We had trouble with the radio so we elected to fly the test flight without it. After settling in to the cockpit and carrying out all the necessary checks I engaged the starter, and soon got the first cough and the shake of the big old Merlin engine as it began to come to life. Next, I flipped on the mag switch to both and the engine settled down to a nice idle. Chocks out, brakes off, I taxied to the end of the runway. I did a very thorough run-up, checking the mags, doing a power check, prop control check, double checking all the trim tabs for proper setting, and the fuel selector valve: all standard procedures for any flight.

Before taxiing on to the runway I went over my plan of action should the engine fail on or after take off. Then I taxied the aircraft out on to the runway and I looked down at that long nose with the big propeller spinning in front of me and thought how lucky I am. After a cursory glance around I pushed up on the power and at the sound of the Merlin engine, the blood started to rush! I released the brakes, increased the power, and the aircraft smoothly accelerated down the runway. At about 50mph the tail slowly came up and by then I had take off power on the engine; in this case I used 50in and 3,000rpm. Accelerating to about 100mph I slowly lifted the airplane into the air. The aircraft was flawless and running very smoothly—not a miss, not a shake, as I ascended into the cloudy skies at Danville.

After take off, I made a climbing turn around

The N51BS is inspected after first flight by Mike "there must be some oil in there somewhere" VadeBonCoeur.

Despite Mike's searching, not a drop of leaking fluid was found. Paul Coggan

over the top of the airport and climbed to 7,500ft and leveled off. I continuously checked all the instruments for proper readings and reduced the power to an economical setting of about 32in and 2,350rpm while allowing all the temperatures to stabilize. I made a few turns left and right while continuing to stay over the top of the airport.

After determining that all the temperatures were remaining normal and the oil pressure was stable, I began to make some steeper turns left and right, eventually slowing the aircraft down to a slow flight configuration to the approach of stall up to the buffet point and then full stalls. In addition, I did some G-turns as I pulled into the buffet. All the temperatures and systems were quite normal so I did a few rolls, another stall or two, dived the Mustang to 450mph, and continued to circle just to put some time on the engine.

About an hour later I slowly started to descend towards the airport. As I came around on final for some reason I couldn't seem to figure out how to get the aircraft down on the runway so I had to make a fly-by. Of course, at legal speeds and altitudes, so I came back around again and made the overhead and set the beautiful machine back on the runway. As I taxied up I was greeted by several people, all with grins from ear to ear.

I unstrapped and climbed out of the plane telling Butch that if Mike ever needed a job to come to Fort Wayne, Indiana and we would put him to work. There was not a single squawk on the first test flight. It was my 21st test flight in a Mustang and one of the most pleasant ever made in the type. It will be a memory that I will cherish for the rest of my life.

Thank you, Butch, for giving me the honor and privilege of making the first test flight in *Lil' Margaret*.

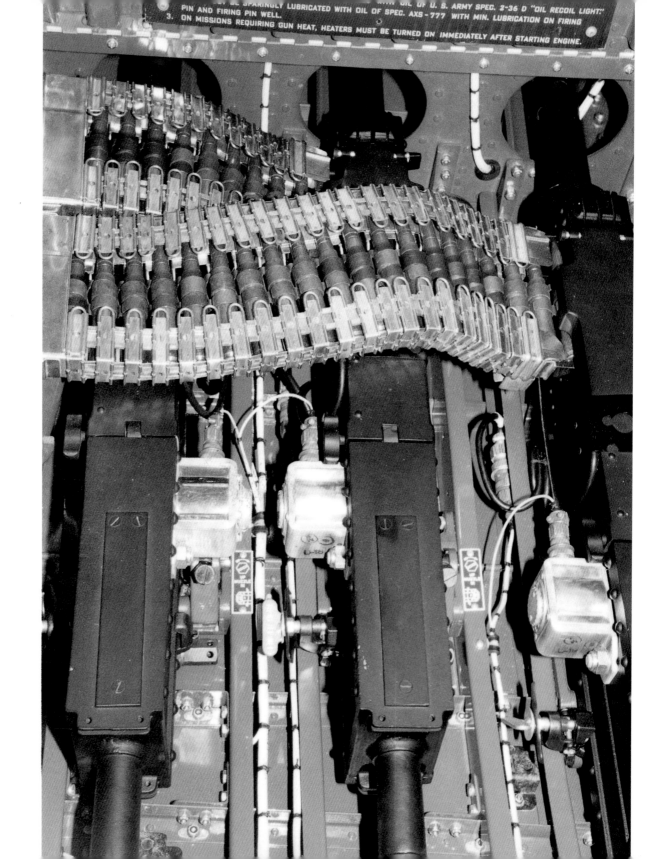

Chapter Four

Final Details

What about the paint scheme? Mike explained in detail, "It was decided early on in the project that the aircraft would be rolled out as close as possible to the original when it emerged from the NAA factory. This meant painting the wings, but having a natural metal fuselage (in our case highly polished). Silver paint is notoriously difficult to shoot and at the time I had very little experience painting. I'd certainly never painted an area this big before. So I was concerned about shooting a single stage IMRON on the Mustang wing—being metallic there can be problems with striping and the metals not flowing properly. I'd seen several beautiful paint jobs from many shops and knew I couldn't achieve that. We wanted the polyurethane paint—the most durable available—but there was none available in

Butch Schroeder stripping the masking from around the USAF national insignia. Markings and stencils were applied directly to the polished surface. Mike VadeBonCoeur

Close-up of one of the gun bays with ammunition chute feeds being fitted. Mike VadeBonCoeur

Installation of the fuselage fuel tank was not easy, but was done by the book. The tank cannot be used, and in any event would cause the cen- *ter of gravity problems experienced by many D model Mustang pilots in combat.* Mike VadeBonCoeur

a base coat/clear coat. That was until our DuPont representative told us that they had just released the IMRON 5000 and 6000 series paints. However, these were for fleet applications on trucks and buses which put us off a little at first. After further discussion, they talked us into it. The idea is that the base coat silver is sprayed to get an overall coverage and as it goes on it appears dull. Then you quickly apply the clear coat which is exactly what we wanted. I wouldn't be afraid to use the paint

again. We don't have a paint booth in the hangar so we made a makeshift unit. The fuselage star and bar and the wing paint are both IMRON 5000—the rest of the components were done in a single stage IMRON which is available here locally. Originally, the front thirty percent of the wing had a thick dark red bondo type material applied to build up the profile, and this was removed by Butch when he stripped the wings (anyone that has stripped this filler off a set of Mustang wings will remember it—as the paint stripper works it softens the filler which drops off like thick treacle). We elected not to fill the seams—it just wasn't practical. We also elected not to have heavy paint coverage. Some of the paint schemes we'd seen hide seams, rivets, and generally detail on the skin. We didn't want that—we preferred a neat, military-looking paint application. There are some special marks on the port wing and also the port canopy rail to aid the pilot get pictures from the cameras accurately. Fortunately, the details for these are all in the maintenance manuals. They were simple to apply. We also located drawings which showed all the stencils all over the aircraft. There is a tremendous amount of stenciling to do. Some of it is black, some red, and interestingly some orange stencils on the prop. It will look very colorful and many people may question its authenticity. Of course we don't know if the aircraft originally had all these stencils when it left the factory, but the wings still had the stenciling when Butch acquired them so they certainly did. A lot of the markings on the aircraft looked like they were rubber stamped. We figured enough was enough, as it would not be practical to have rubber stamps made for every stencil! Mike was later to find out from Hess Bomberger that some of these markings were actually water soluble decals that were applied and then protected with a clear coat treatment. Banaire in California made the stencils for the project. As they had done the T-6 for us some years ago we just provided the sizes and the wording and they did all our stencils for us, and agreed to do it for the F-6D. As we had the aircraft microfiche drawings, we looked up all the stencil marks and details for

decals, stamps, and all the other markings. Some of the stencils were on the inside and would not normally be seen, but we knew they were there so good enough—on they went!" It is obvious that the aircraft would be painted as it was assembled to ensure good corrosion protection internally as well as externally, but it was decided that the final stenciling and nose art should be applied after the first flight.

Guns

In recent years there has been a trend towards installing replica guns in warbirds. The N51BS *Lil' Margaret* is no exception. Mike outlined the process "We received the guns from Jay Wisler. After some consideration we stripped them down and sandblasted the parts, repainting the aluminum parts matte black. We already had the metal mounts and these were all stripped and

The guns and linkage during a trial fitting in the port wing. Mike VadeBonCoeur

gun-blued. The ammunition was another interesting exercise. We purchased all the D links and linked them together ourselves—we bought a linking machine from Jay Wisler—to do the job. We actually have original solenoids for the guns and the original gun heaters. All these are wired so you can sit in the cockpit, squeeze the trigger, and the solenoids will click—and why not. It was just as easy to run the wiring and have them working. Butch picked up the feed chutes some time ago. It would have been nice to have six original Browning .50 calibers in there but it wasn't to be, so…"

There are two wiring systems for the guns, so the pilot could keep firing if one was battle damaged. One comes from the front side of the wing through the wheel wells, and the other along the rear spar just forward of the flaps. Had the guns been real rather than replicas, they could be fired as all the support equipment works. On the original D model Mustang 400 rounds were carried for the inboard guns

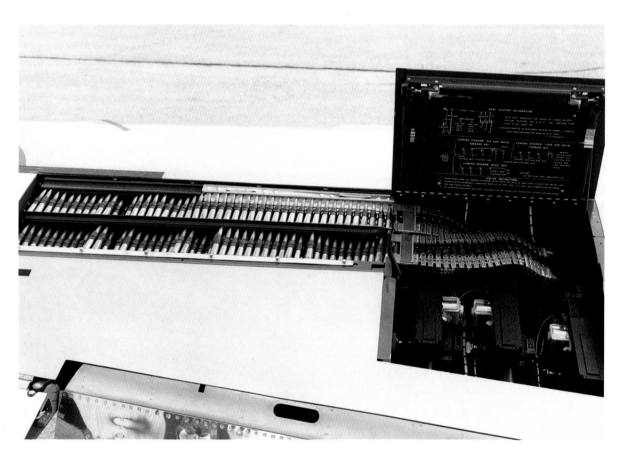

The finished gun bays complete with ammunition (inert of course) and all the chutes and links in place. Note the bore-sighting information placard inside the gun bay doors. Mike Vade-BonCouer

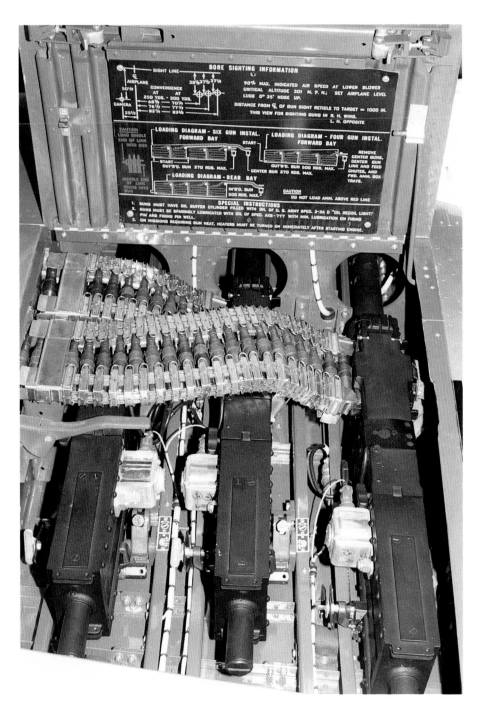

A close up of the gun bay doors showing the bore sighting information placard. Mike VadeBon-Coeur

The cockpit shot from underneath before the wings and fuselage were mated. Note the detail on the rudder pedals and the new hardware.

By this time the armor-plated firewall had been fitted.

and 270 rounds for the center and outboard weapons. The gun mounts were adjustable and were standard bore-sighted at 300 yards forward of the barrels. An original N1 gun camera was also installed in the leading edge of the port wing root. Though it clicks and buzzes they are still trying to locate film and get it to work.

Cockpit

The cockpit was changed a little from the original. Originally, the metal floor was covered with non-slip coated plywood. For the sake of appearance and to avoid getting the non-slip grit all over the place, they elected to varnish the wood and install stainless steel kick plates.

Butch also purchased and installed a K14 gunsight. It is a "C" model, a later version and a little different from the World War II model, but they knew it would work. It is fully functional; it will be really neat to have Butch fly around with it operating! The cockpit of *Lil' Margaret* is signif-

Spaghetti anyone? The myriad of wires looks like gobbledygook to most of us, but Mike Vade-BonCoeur managed to wire the aircraft with few problems but speaks highly of telephone assistance offered by Fort Wayne Air Service. Mike VadeBonCoeur

Right
Mike and Butch initially discussed mocking up the armor plate in aluminum but decided to reinstall original armor plate despite the weight penalty. The fuel tank is installed below the aircraft radio equipment, immediately behind the pilot.

icantly different from that found in other Mustangs. Today's air traffic environment is very different from the European theater in World War II where the P-51D saw the majority of its combat service. Modern avionics dominate modern Mustang cockpits with LORAN, satellite navigation systems, and computerized fuel flow controls all being the norm. Many owners prefer to get away from the standard North American cockpit green paint and have a more modern, ergonomic light grey paint scheme. Butch and Mike opted to use cockpit green and keep *Lil' Margaret* as original as possible.

In the F-6D, all the camera controls are

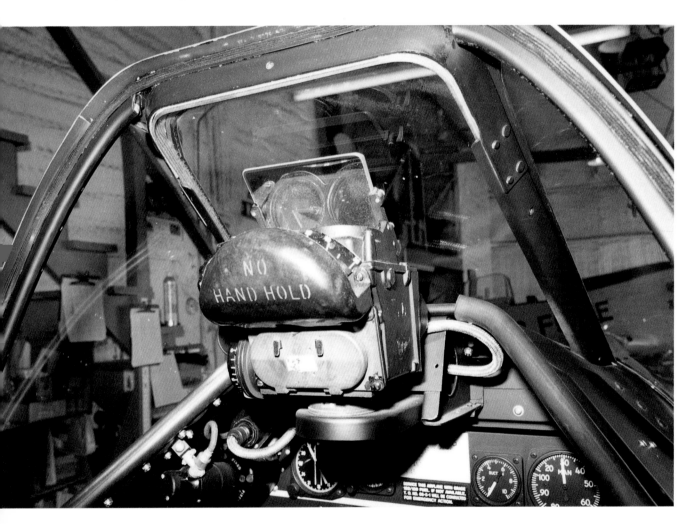

The K-14 gunsight shortly after initial installation. This is an original unit particularly impressed each of the four legendary Mustang Aces that sat in the aircraft at Oshkosh in 1993.

Fuel tank controls and utilities panel, all original items except the placards. Mike VadeBon-Coeur

A close look at the elevator trim wheel. Again, original coloring and cockpit equipment (almost all of which is functional) impressed all the Mustang pilots that have graced the cockpit since the rebuild was finished. Mike VadeBonCoeur

Not only have all exterior parts of the aircraft been stenciled and marked, all of the components underneath the skin have been correctly color coordinated and stenciled as well. Mike VadeBonCoeur

Left
Throttle control and placards. Note camera control panel, which is unique to the North American F-6D and K models. Mike VadeBonCoeur

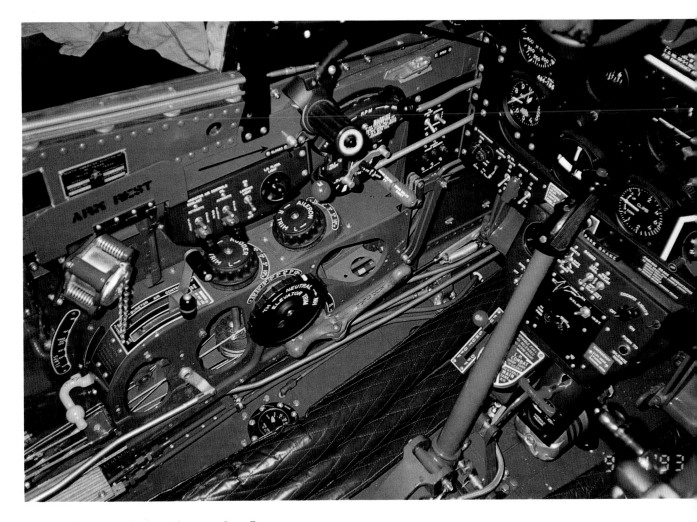

The cockpit just before the wooden floor was installed.

original and the gun controls activate the replica Browning .50cal guns (which cannot fire, though if real guns had been installed they would fire because all the support equipment is in place). Though the fuel tanks are functional and plumbed they cannot be jettisoned in the air as this is against FAA regulations.

The original radios were detailed exter-nally and new rubber mounts fitted. Butch and Mike elected not to have them work-ing—there are problems with frequency bleed on the old radios anyway—but they are wired to appear functional. Also installed are modern King KX155 units and a North Star LORAN as well as an encod-ing transponder. It is installed below the original radio switches and is concealed by

a canvas cover on the ground so you cannot see the installation. The only hint of non-originality in the cockpit is the VOR head in the instrument panel and this occupies a slot that was blanked off in the military. "All our information on the cockpit came from original NAA photos and flight manuals," Mike added. The author supplied some original NAA photographs that he was fortunate to be given by Rockwell when they had someone keen enough to care about those old North American airplanes.

What about the general structure? Mike went on to say, "One of the ribs in the tail cone was pretty untidy. It had been repaired several times and had major patching. Gerry Beck at Tri-State Air Service provided us with a replacement from stock with a modification to accommodate the camera attach plus the cable routing. It fit like a charm and we were extremely pleased with it."

Cockpit seat finished, painted, trimmed, and ready for installation. Note bucket seat and harness fittings. Mike VadeBonCoeur

Left
The wooden floor and stainless steel kick plates in place. Mike VadeBonCoeur

Chapter Five

The EAA Convention at Oshkosh

After I had left Danville, just a few weeks before the annual Oshkosh convention and fly in, final preparations had been put into action. Already the Mustang's metal skin had been lovingly polished, yet there was still more to come. The final stencils had been painstakingly applied, with much work still to come to bring this piece of aviation history up to the standard where Butch felt it would win the World War II Grand Champion award. It was the details that the judges would be looking for, the bits and pieces that most modern Mustangs shed, and the authenticity. I have been privileged over the years to see many Mustangs in various states of rebuild, many of them worked to an exceptionally high standard. I secretly knew that the judges at EAA would not be disappointed with this airplane. The Experimental Air-

craft Association's Warbirds of America has a prestigious awards system which has been running now for many years. It has promoted a high standard of rebuilding and restoration and the awards are much sought after.

The EAA Warbirds of America awards have a set of judging standards which are simple and allow consistent and fair competition between common and exotic and between complex and simple warbird types. It is widely acknowledged that winning an EAA award adds to the market value of an airplane, and the judging standards aim to provide a standard that is fair to all entrants. It is interesting to note that the underlying purpose of the EAA awards scheme is "to improve the breed by stimulating competition." Authenticity is encouraged, but safety is paramount and aircraft are not marked down for an item essential to its safe operation but which may not be original. The judging standards also emphasize that no consideration is given to which organization, individual, or museum accomplished the restoration, or of its cost. Essen-

The auxiliary fuel tank and guns both look authentic and use original fittings and hardware wherever possible. Edward Toth, Jr.

Nose artwork is applied to the Mustang. Mike VadeBonCoeur

tially, the awards are designed to recognize the workmanship of the restorer, either a professional or a warbird owner. For the World War II award (which is the award *Lil' Margaret* won), the aircraft in this category must have had an equivalent type aircraft operational in military service between September 1, 1939, and July 26, 1945.

The judges are selected by the Chairman of Warbird Judging and must be members of EAA Warbirds of America in good standing. They all have a thorough knowledge of the aircraft types to be judged—this knowledge having been gained through personal experience, and this includes historical research qualifications. So each judge knows exactly what he is looking for.

In each case, the aircraft owner is encouraged to be present at the judging, not only to open the cockpit and remove access panels but also to answer any questions the judges may have on the restoration of the aircraft, its history, technical specifications, etc. Additionally most owners present a book of photographs which show the airplane throughout the restoration process, which are invaluable for showing the work that went into the project. The book can also show information on the historical research carried out, photographs of the aircraft in military service (where available), and very often these act to validate the authenticity of the paint scheme. Also, and on a positive note, owners are encouraged to ask each judge what they should aim for to make the aircraft "a better and more competitive restoration."

So how does the judging work? Each judge inspects the aircraft entered in the competition and awards a point score. Scores are totaled by individual judges and then averaged. The score must be a minimum of 80 points before the aircraft is reckoned to be eligible for an award in any category (Best P-51, Best T-6, Best Jet etc.) and it is widely acknowledged that the award is so prestigious that awards should not be made "where a sufficiently outstanding aircraft—eighty points or more—is not entered." Obviously to do so would diminish the significance of the much sought after EAA award.

Judging

As related earlier, it is the aim of EAA Warbirds of America to preserve, in original flying condition, aircraft important to the military heritage of the United States. Authenticity therefore is an important consideration, and judges are told to give credit to restorations that incorporate original equipment such as bomb racks, guns, gun sights, radios, operational gun turrets, and original cockpit configurations. However,

A photo reconnaissance version of the P-51D, the F-6D Lil' Margaret *as it appeared at the Oshkosh show, where it won the 1993 World War II Grand Champion award.* Edward Toth, Jr.

The attention to detail on Lil' Margaret *carried over to the stenciling and decal work. Note camera port and stenciling of pilot Clyde B. East and crew on the canopy. Edward Toth, Jr.*

marks are not subtracted for modifications which enhance the operational safety of the aircraft like more efficient brakes, additional radio or navigation equipment more able to aid the pilot in negotiating today's complex air traffic environment, better instrument lighting, and improved safety and warning systems.

Once judging of individual aircraft has taken place and the scores tallied and averaged, the difficulty factor is then taken into account. EAA recognizes that it is very difficult for example to compare a restoration of a T-6 trainer to that of a B-25 Mitchell bomber when considering both for Grand Champion awards. With this in mind each aircraft type is allocated a difficulty factor points score which is then added to the total score when comparing dissimilar aircraft for an award for which they are both eligible. These are as follows:

One point: L-1, L-2, L-5, L-18, PT-19, PT-22
Two points: BT-13, Stearman, N3N, L-13, L-19, LC-126, O-1, T-41
Three points: O-2, T-34
Four points: C-45, T-6, UC-78
Five points: F-3F, P-39, P-40, P-51, P-63, F8F, F6F, F4F, Spitfire, Corsair, P-47, TBM
Seven points: Pinto jet, Sea Fury, T-28, Vampire
Eight points: F-86, P-38, P-80, P-82, T-33, T- 37, F9F Panther, Skyraider
Nine points: A-4,A-20, B-23, B-25, B-26, C-46, C-47, C-117, F-4, PBY, T-38
Ten points (maximum): B-17, B-24, B-29, B-50, C-54, C-69, C-118, C-121
Aircraft not covered by the above table are assigned a difficulty factor by the judges.

Before the difficulty factor comes into play, the plane is judged in the following categories:

Authenticity: Plus points only—no points are deducted for parts that are not authentic. Primary attention to external details, paint schemes, etc. No deduction for necessary modernization of radio equipment and systems. Points are also allocated for details such as guns, bombs, bomb racks, gunsights, original cockpit fixtures, panel layout, etc. to a maximum of fifteen points.

General appearance: This covers the aircraft in its entirety; workmanship, cleanliness, maintenance, and overall appeal. The paint scheme should be appropriate for type and model. For example, a Navy T-28 or SNJ should be consistent with the period, and the squadron insignia, etc., should correspond to assigned ship, command, etc. However, the plane need not represent an exact copy of a previous warbird but can be painted as a representative of that time period (*Lil' Margaret* is painted to represent the aircraft flown by Clyde East, although it is not the actual aircraft flown by him). There are no deductions for gloss paint as this is an example of an item which improves aircraft maintenance. The warbirds are flying aircraft and are judged as such; there is no deduction for the normal amount of dirt and soil accumulated in obvious use. Maximum fifteen points.

Fuselage: Cleanliness, workmanship, interior details, wiring, painting interior and exterior, control cables, safety of flight items, etc. If possible the judges should view the fuselage interior for quality of restoration. It is the owner's prerogative to remove or not to remove inspection covers. The owners are urged to cooperate, however, since the inside of the fuselage is the major portion of the restoration of an aircraft. Maximum fifteen points.

Safety items: Parachutes (three points); shoulder harness (two points for each occupant); internal and hand-held fire bottles (two points); helmet (two points); Nomex flight suit (one point); Nomex gloves (one point); miscellaneous additional safety equipment such as operational ejection seats, warning circuits for the engine and aircraft systems (2 points); first aid kit (2 points). When a safety item is not appropriate for the type of aircraft being judged (such as parachutes in some L-birds or ejection seats in piston-powered trainers) the aircraft is awarded the points for that item. Nomex flight suits, gloves, shoulder harnesses, fire bottles, and first aid kits would be appropriate in any aircraft regardless of whether or not the aircraft had them originally. Maximum fifteen points.

Cockpit: Workmanship, detail, cleanliness; necessary, proper and operating instrumentation, placards, markings, wiring harnesses, cockpit layout, lighting, etc. Maximum ten points.

Engine and accessory section: Cleanliness, workmanship, safety of flight items, proper safe tying, cotter pins, linkages, lines and hoses in good repair. Maximum ten points.

Landing gear and wheel wells: Cleanliness, workmanship, routing of hoses and lines, condition of tires, brakes etc. Maximum ten points.

Wings and tail surfaces: Workmanship, painting, cleanliness, safety of flight items. Maximum ten points.

Difficulty points: Difficulty points are assigned as per the list above. They are

The F-6D Lil' Margaret *in it's element.* Edward Toth, Jr.

World War II Mustang Ace Bruce Carr, who has since flown a Mustang solo again after a training course with Stallion '51 in Florida, congratulates Mike VadeBonCoeur on the Golden Wrench Award made by the EAA and sponsored by Snap-on-Tools. Beth VadeBonCoeur

Famed Mustang Ace and test pilot Chuck Yeager with Dave, Mike, and Butch. Beth VadeBonCoeur

used only when the judges are comparing dissimilar types that are in contention for the same award, i.e. Grand Champion, Reserve Grand Champion, Third place runner up, and past Grand Champion award. All aircraft of the same type receive the same difficulty factor. For example, all T-6s receive +4 points. It is interesting to note that a perfect score is 100, plus the difficulty points when applicable.

The scores for the same aircraft as determined by each judge will be totaled and the Grand Champion should be the plane with the highest overall total score including difficulty points. Reserve Grand Champion has the second highest and so forth. In the Best of Type category, the example of the type with the highest overall score wins (Best T-6, Best P-51, etc.).

A Word From Peter Moll

I talked with Peter Moll, executive director of EAA Warbirds of America, about the award which was won by *Lil' Margaret* in 1993, and the EAA's philosophy behind the award scheme. Peter explained that EAA regards safety in flight as paramount, and preserving the airframes for future generations is equally important. So the judges are not only looking for the points outlined in the judging guidelines, but also for items that will prolong the aircraft's life.

So where did *Lil' Margaret* score? Peter told me "The F-6D is a rare airplane, and this was a good starting point—you do not see many F-6s out there. Not only had Butch and his team installed all the guns and the cameras, but he had taken the trouble to trace and paint on all the markings, the stencils, and special reference marks on the wings. I thought that the tail warning radar was outstanding—you just do not see these items any more! Another point that I liked, and I know the judges did too, was the fact that the fuselage was not painted, and it appeared just as it did in the war, though obviously they did not polish the aluminum skin as highly. He also went to the trouble of locating and replicating a real paint scheme, and finding the pilot that flew the original airplane to get his impression of the restoration. That for us was really above and beyond what he needed to do.

"I think what Butch's airplane did was set a standard, a good standard, and since then we have seen people go that extra mile to achieve authenticity. Though Butch took his time, he went all out for authenticity and the result was a truly magnificent airplane and as a result we have seen more people follow his example. So instead of simply producing an authentic paint scheme and doing some internal details in order just to try and win an award at Oshkosh, he has encouraged others to do the job well. Our judges have also started to get real picky, opening up access panels and probing the tiniest accessible spaces to see the work that has been done, to see if the airplane has been restored, and all the while bearing in the philosophy that we want to see aircraft preserved for future generations, and to keep them flying." Peter also commented on the increasingly high standards of restoration now being seen including the use of flat paint, a process pioneered by Dick Hansen and Dan Caldarale (and also the Fighter Collection in the U.K.) which is more accurate than gloss paint in some areas.

Presentation of the award at the Fond du Lac Holiday Inn. Butch holds the Grand Champion trophy and Mike has the Golden Wrench Award. David Young came on board two years from the end of the project but had worked with his father, Bob Young of Young's Airframe Repair—both made a significant contribution to the metal skin work on N51BS.

So what other points did the judges like on *Lil' Margaret*? "Specifically, the diamond tread tires, and especially the underwing drop tanks. They are really rare these days and super authentic and it was just marvelous to see these features."

So although the job to restore the F-6D *Lil' Margaret* was a long and arduous one, Butch and Mike and the other people involved achieved their aim and made their own personal mark in aviation history.

A Brief History of the Mustang

The History of North American Aviation's finest piston fighter is well documented, though some controversy still surrounds the history of evolution of the type. However, to put this story into context we will review events leading up to the first flight of the North American NA-73X on 26 October 1940. In his book *Mustang: A Documentary History,* author Jeff Ethell put forward a number of (then) new ideas on the history of the P-51. Though some of the facts put forward by Ethell are still disputed today (some of them by people actually involved in the design and production of the type), many historians accept the Ethell version as accurate mainly due to the sheer amount of documentary evidence and modern day interviews carried out by him.

Much credit for the development of the North American Mustang (and thus to the F-6D, the subject of this book) must be given to the U.S. Army Air Corps, and particularly to Colonel Oliver Echols. One of the great strengths of the AAC in the thirties was the freedom they were allowed in acquiring experimental aircraft types, the Mustang amongst them. Despite the lethargic attitude toward fighter development prevailing in the thirties, it was the AAC, and in particular Echols who pushed forward development of such legendary types as the XP-38, XP-39, and XP-40.

Despite the fact that the AAC had the freedom to produce up to fourteen examples of any given project type before they had to approach Congress for funding, such funding was (as is the case today) always limited. In spite of this restriction Echols most certainly used this facility to push forward development of front line fighters to the extent that when war did break out the air power picture in the USA was comparatively healthy, largely as a result of Echols and his associates activities. Another individual that was to play a key role in the original Mustang specification was Lt. Benjamin Kelsey, who headed the office controlling the experimental and production pursuit projects office at Wright Field.

After the Nazi invasion of Poland in the

Some seventeen North American P-51Ds being made ready for ground running engine trials at the Inglewood plant in California. NAA publicity photo

fall of 1939, both French and British armament purchasing teams headed for the United States. It was the P-40 that initially attracted their attention and buying power and by the turn of the year both countries had ordered maximum numbers of the type. It should be remembered at this stage that the XP-40 was, put simply, an inline-engined development of the radial engine Curtiss Hawk, the P-36. While Kelsey was pushing hard for the next generation in the Curtiss fighter line (which was on the drawing board as early as 1938), the powers that be at the AAC would not allow the time required to build the XP-46. The truth of the matter was that the war machine was moving ahead at a rate that demanded aircraft and machinery to counter the German war machine.

The turning point in the Mustang's development came in late 1939 when the British Purchasing Commission began to look for companies in the United States willing to build the Curtiss P-40 under

Thirty-five North American Aviation Mustangs
(P-51Bs and Cs) being made ready for ferrying
after test flying. NAA publicity picture

license. It was Echols who suggested the Commission look for a manufacturer that had the capacity to manufacture a new fighter: Curtiss and the AAC would then make available the data from the XP-46 to assist them.

North American Aviation at Inglewood were employed in building the North American Harvard and T-6 for the French and the British when they were approached by the head of the New York-based British Purchasing Commission, Sir Henry Self, in 1939 to license build the P-40. NAA rejected the proposals outright. But Self was excited at the prospect of the latest research data being made available for the production of a new fighter to supersede the P-40 and made a personal approach to James H. Dutch Kindelburger with a repeat proposal centered on license building the P-40 or designing a new fighter based on the XP-46 research and wind tunnel data. Again the former proposal was rejected, but Kindelberger was much happier to consider the latter proposal. From here onwards things moved fairly quickly, culminating in a formal contract between NAA and the British/French Purchasing commissions for 400 aircraft designated NA-73. The new fighter was designed utilizing the XP-46 research data which had been purchased from Curtiss by NAA for some

A North American Aviation A-36A dive-bomber version of the famous fighter. The A-36 was used widely in Italy on dive-bombing missions but was not as successful as the P-51 as a fighter. NAA

$56,000. Previously, on the May 4th 1940 NAA had signed a joint agreement with the Army Air Corps which amounted to a release for the foreign sale of the new fighter—the NA-73.

It was at this point that Raymond Rice, NAA's Chief Engineer, **began to** get the project under way.

Much has been written about the laminar flow wing and its contribution toward the success of the Mustang project. Basically, in June 1939, the U.S.-based National Advisory Committee for Aeronautics (NACA) at Langley Field, Virginia, released the research data under a confidential classification. Ed Horkey, who was working on the NA-73 aerodynamics under the aerodynamics engineering chief Larry Waite, became sold on the idea that this new wing section would contribute significantly to the new fighter's performance.

The North American team were now working very long hours, seven days a week, on the new fighter. At this time the only relatively high-powered liquid-cooled engine available for the new fighter was

The Mustang was most famous for its service with the USAAF's mighty 8th Air Force. A 354th FG razorback Mustang is seen here being *prepared for an escort mission in 1944. via Gordon Hunsberger*

the V-1710 Allison engine and this was selected for installation in the NA-73. Contrary to popular belief, until Jeff Ethell's research pointed out otherwise, the British Purchasing Commissions did not determine a 120-day limit on the contract—January 1941 was mentioned for the initial delivery and 30 September the same year for contract completion.

To summarize, the team at NAA had taken the aerodynamic research from the XP-46 and, combining it with a laminar flow wing all under the pressure of wartime, had produced an aircraft that would become one (if not the) finest piston-engined fighter aircraft ever produced.

North American engineers pushed out the NA-73X in just 102 days, utilizing much existing systems from the T-6s they were building including electrics, hydraulics wheels, and brakes. Just twenty days after roll out the engine arrived, and after installation, the aircraft flew for the first time on October 26, 1940 with freelance test pilot Vance Breese at the controls. Just before the NA-73X flew the British had placed another order for 300 more aircraft. On December 9, 1940 the NA-73-series airplanes were named Mustang.

With momentum gaining, the Mustang production commenced and the first production aircraft (serial number AG345) made its maiden flight on April 23, 1941 with Louis Wait at the controls. Next on the line, AG346, was the first aircraft to be shipped to the UK arriving just one year after the maiden flight of the NA-73X. It was assembled and test flown from Speke airport close to Liverpool. Due to the relatively poor high altitude performance of the V-1710 powered Mustang, the RAF were quick to assign the new aircraft to Army

North American Aviation test pilot Robert C. Chilton flew all models of the P-51 and amassed several thousand hours test flying on type. NAA

Co-operation Command for tactical reconnaissance and low level attack duties. There were a number of operational problems with the early Mustangs including cooling and engine overheating.

Running parallel to this activity was the USAAC's own interest in the type. In May 1940 the Army Air Corps had requested the fourth and tenth production aircraft to be made available at Wright Field for flight testing and evaluation. After sanctioning by the Assistant Secretary of War, the two aircraft were transferred and designated XP-51. Many teething troubles and some inefficiencies by AAC personnel on the administrative side caused some delay in introducing the type to the air force.

Though there was a wide mix of enthusiasm and lethargy for the P-51 entering service with the USAAC, there was still much interest in the Mustang at Wright Field where Colonel Echols was pushing hard for an AAF version. Eventually some fifty-five were kept by the AAF as straight

An interesting comparison picture between the lightweight P-51H Mustang (in the foreground) and the stock P-51D. The lightweight P-51H was really only related by name and was a very different aircraft than its predecessor. via William T. Larkins

P-51s (the balance, some ninety-three aircraft, went to the RAF: and, perhaps most important of all, two aircraft were set aside for the XP-78 project—aircraft fitted with Rolls Royce Merlin engines manufactured by Packard). In the meantime the Mustang was still being built and some of the aircraft were diverted to the A-36 production line. Put very simply, the addition of dive brakes and bomb racks to the airframe made it into an A-36 (first flown by Bob Chilton on 21st September 1942), which quickly proved itself as an effective dive bomber—however this aspect is beyond the scope of this condensed history. It was at

this time that the Mustang was first used as a photo recconaissance version: F-6As were in operation by March 1943 with several units including 111 and 154 Squadrons of the 68th Observation Group. Beginning in December 1943, F-6Bs of the 9th Air Force (converted P-51As from the UK), operated some 25 aircraft for seven months, performing sterling recce work in preparation for the Allied invasion of continental Europe. The F-6A was also in service in Italy with the 111th TRS.

In April 1942 the AFDU was evaluating the Mustang I. This led to Rolls-Royce test pilot Ronald Harker being allowed to fly one of the two test aircraft (AG422). After some flight testing, Harker was convinced of the airframes potential and after some consultations requested a Merlin 61 power-plant be mated to the low drag Mustang airframe. Initially, the request met with opposition and even hostile comments. After further negotiation with the British Air Ministry, three aircraft were approved for transfer to the Nottinghamshire Rolls Royce airfield located at Hucknall. Friendly rivalry emerged as Rolls Royce moved to install their Merlins in several airframes across the pond, while North American had a Packard-built Merlin made available for installation in one of their airframes. In the U.S., P-51 41-37352 was the first of two aircraft converted to take the engine, flying for the first time on November 30, 1942 when Bob Chilton took the aircraft into the air for forty-five minutes at Inglewood, California. In all, five Mustangs were earmarked in the U.K. for conversion to the Merlin. On 13th October 1942 Rolls Royce pilot Ron Shepherd got airborne in AL975 for a half-hour maiden flight. Amidst this feverish

The majority of early civilian Mustangs came from a batch surplused by the Royal Canadian Air Force. Today's Mustang population still consists of a large number of ex-RCAF air-frames. Jerry Vernon

An interesting photograph showing a P-51D on its nose following a landing accident after a combat mission with the 8th Air Force. Mustang propellers are still a much sought after item today for obvious reasons, and can cost as much as $60,000 each. via Jerry Scutts

activity and the exchange of information between NAA and Rolls Royce the USAAF had already placed an order for some 400 P-51B Mustangs. A much larger order was placed even before the Merlin-powered aircraft had taken to the air when 1350 Mustangs (Dallas built and designated C models) were ordered. So after a slow start North American's finest was off the blocks.

Once the final P-51B specification had been finalized, the AAF and North American did not waste any more time in pushing out the first production model. Bob Chilton flew it for the first time on May 5, 1943. And so the story continued with the P-51B being seen as the answer to the USAAC's long range bomber escort requirements. Though the Merlin-powered Mustang had its fair share of troubles it went into service relatively smoothly compared to its contemporaries. The XP-51D, essentially a P-51B with a cut down rear fuselage and bubble canopy flew for the first time on November 17, 1943. To many this was the one—it looked right, handled right. It was RIGHT! The P-51D formed the basis for the F-6K and F-6D models, the latter being the subject of this story.

It would be imprudent however, not to put this condensed history into perspective by listing some of the aircraft's achievements. In the European theater alone Mustangs flew 213,873 missions amassing over 1,120,000 flying hours. In contrast some 62,607 tactical support missions were flown with the loss of over 350 aircraft. The Mustang was responsible for shooting down 4,950 enemy aircraft and destroying over 4,000 more on the ground; overall statistics show that the Mustang claimed 13 kills for every 100 sorties flown; an impressive record for a fighting aircraft.

The Mustang also served in Korea. A pair of P-51D-30NA models are pictured here with the South African Air Force. via Jerry Scutts

Mustang Specifications

North American built 7,956 P-51Ds in Inglewood, California, and Dallas, Texas. All were powered by Packard-built Merlin V-1650 engines.

Wingspan:.........................37ft
Length:.......................32ft 3in
Height:.....................13ft 8in
Wing area ....233ft^2

Gross weight 10,100lb
Empty weight..................7,125lb
Max. T.O. weight..............11,600lb

Max. speed ....437mph at 25,000ft
Landing speed.................100mph

Climb to 30,000ft 13min
Service ceiling 41,900ft
Max. range 2300mi
Max. fuel.....................489gal

Index